ARTISAN CARAMELS

SANDY AREVALO

FRONT TABLE BOOKS

AN IMPRINT OF CEDAR FORT, INC.

SPRINGVILLE, UTAH

ISBN: 978-1-4621-1442-9

Published by Front Table Books, an imprint of Cedar Fort, Inc.
2373 W. 700 S., Springville, UT, 84663
Distributed by Cedar Fort, Inc., www.cedarfort.com

Library of Congress Cataloging-in-Publication Data

Arevalo, Sandy, 1975- author.
Artisan caramels / Sandy Arevalo.
    pages cm
 ISBN 978-1-4621-1442-9 (acid-free paper)
 1. Cooking (Caramel) I. Title.
 TX767.C37A74 2014
 641.6--dc23
                          2014019027

Cover and page design by Bekah Claussen
Cover design © 2014 by Lyle Mortimer
Edited by Rachel Munk

Printed in the United States of America

10 9 8 7 6 5 4 3 2 1

FOR MIGUEL, CONNOR, AND ADDISON.
MY WORLD IS A SWEETER PLACE BECAUSE OF YOU.

CONTENTS

INTRODUCTION

I want to say that my passion for caramel was instantaneous—That I tried a recipe, fell in love, and the rest was history. But that wasn't the case.

I was so afraid of burning my first batch of caramel. In the end, I didn't cook it long enough. My final result was a caramel so runny I couldn't even cut it!

Disaster followed in my second attempt when the oil separated from the sugar.

Several more recipes followed, as did several more failed attempts. I had boil-overs, burnt pans, and caramel so hard it required a sledge hammer to break it apart. It was out of sheer determination, and what had now become a mild obsession, that led to my creation of a perfect caramel.

It turns out that, despite its four basic ingredients, caramel can be quite temperamental. You need to pay attention to it. It can be a matter of seconds between undercooked and overcooked. It can burn easily and boil furiously. But for all the time that is required to make it, there is no greater reward than biting into that beautiful, golden, chewy, artisan caramel.

INGREDIENTS AND TOOLS

BASIC INGREDIENTS

HEAVY CREAM

Also called heavy whipping cream.

CORN SYRUP

For most recipes, use light corn syrup, which is made with vanilla. Dark corn syrup is made with molasses and is better for recipes like stout and pretzel or pfeffernüsse.

SUGAR

White granulated sugar, also known as cane sugar, is preferred in all of these recipes.

BUTTER

Always use unsalted butter.

ADDITIONAL INGREDIENTS FOR FLAVORING

These will vary by recipe. (In the step-by-step, we will make Salted Vanilla Bean caramels with these flavors.)

VANILLA

Use a good-quality vanilla for a stronger flavor. I prefer the vanilla that has flecks of vanilla bean seeds mixed in. The seeds add no real additional flavor, but they look pretty.

SALT

If you like an added crunch, I suggest using a coarse sea salt.

TOOLS

8-QUART STOCK POT

An 8-quart pot may seem large, but larger is better as it will help prevent the caramel from boiling over. Use stainless steel or ceramic coated pots, not Teflon or other non-stick coating. After extended use over such high heat, the coating breaks down and will end up in your caramel.

CANDY THERMOMETER

Don't have one? Get one! You can follow the visual clues of the caramel, but a candy thermometer will tell you exactly when it's ready.

WOODEN SPOON

You will want to use a strong wooden spoon. I have snapped quite a few flimsy handles.

JELLY ROLL PAN

A jelly roll pan is similar to a cookie sheet but has sides. It should be 12.5 x 17.5.

PARCHMENT PAPER

NOT wax paper. The wax on wax paper cannot withstand the heat of the caramel, and could melt or even ignite for recipes that call for the oven.

COOKING SPRAY

I have this listed under tools instead of ingredients, because its real purpose is to prevent caramel from sticking to the pan or the parchment paper, but it does not provide any flavor.

LIQUID MEASURING CUP

A 4-cup measuring cup will be easiest for you, but a 1- or 2-cup will work as well.

MEASURING CUPS

You will mostly need the 1 cup, but some recipes call for a ½ cup.

MEASURING SPOONS

Keep all sizes handy. Liquid flavorings call mostly for the tablespoon, but some of the spices will call for a teaspoon, ½ teaspoon, or ¼ teaspoon.

HELPFUL TIPS

Remove your caramel from the heat once it reaches 248 degrees on a candy thermometer. The caramel will continue to cook as you stir in your flavors. This tip is repeated throughout the book, but it will help prevent you from overcooking your caramel.

Don't walk away from boiling caramel. I cannot stress this enough. It changes so quickly and can be ruined very easily!

I suggest keeping your parchment-lined pan next to your boiling pot. If it happens to start boiling over, you can remove it from the heat and set it on the pan with minimal damage to your stove.

If boiling caramel lands on your stove top, counter top, floor, or baking pan, don't scrub it off. Soak it in hot water until the sugars dissolve, and then clean it with the appropriate cleaners.

The caramel is hot and can splatter when you stir it, especially when you add alcohol-based flavorings such as vanilla. Be careful and wear protective clothing like aprons and long oven gloves. You might want to keep ice water handy in case of burns.

Wait the full time before cutting and wrapping your caramels. Six hours is fine, but eight hours is ideal.

Don't put caramels in the fridge to cool—this will turn them as hard as rocks and will make it really difficult to cut them.

Once caramel is cooled and cut, wrap in parchment or cello wrappers and store in an airtight container in a cool, dry place.

Most caramels, once wrapped, have a shelf life of about three weeks. Caramels wrapped in parchment squares instead of cello wrappers will become stale faster. Caramels with a crust or a topping have a shelf life of one to two weeks.

STEP-BY-STEP CARAMELS

Add your cream, sugar, butter, and corn syrup to your 8-quart stock pot and set over medium-high heat, stirring constantly to incorporate the butter. Your mixture will be a pale yellow/cream color.

Once your caramel starts to boil, it will do so rapidly and furiously. You will notice that the bubbles are small and "fuzzy." Be careful, because this is when it is most likely to get away from you. If you need to look or step away for any reason, set your spoon across the top of the pot; this will help prevent boil-overs.

Keep stirring. You don't have to do it constantly, but do it often to prevent burning.

It will take some time, about 45 minutes, but the caramel will turn golden in color. The bubbles will then be fatter and slower to pop.

It's time to start paying attention to your candy thermometer! The caramel will increase from the "Soft Ball" stage to the "Firm Ball" very quickly!! Once it reaches 248 degrees—that's the line right below firm ball—turn off the heat and quickly stir in the salt and vanilla. Keep in mind that the caramel will continue to cook, even after you have removed it from the heat. The longer you take, the harder the caramel will become.

Pour into a prepared pan.

Allow it to cool for 8 hours.

Remove the caramel from the pan, remove the parchment paper, and cut into squares.

Top with sea salt.

JUST THE BASICS

THESE FOUR FLAVORS WILL HELP YOU GRASP THE BASICS. THEY HAVE LIMITED FLAVORINGS BUT STILL YIELD AMAZING ARTISAN CARAMELS.

SALTED VANILLA BEAN CARAMELS

RICH, BUTTERY CARAMEL TOPPED WITH BEAUTIFUL PIECES OF SEA SALT. PERFECTION DEFINED.

PREPARE YOUR PAN

1. Spray a jelly roll pan with a thin layer of cooking spray. Using a clean, dry paper towel, wipe off the excess. Make sure you cover the sides and bottom of the pan—this will help prevent the caramels from sticking.
2. Trim a piece of parchment paper so that it covers the bottom of the pan, but has about a 2-inch overhang over the handles or sides.
3. Spray the parchment paper again with a light layer of cooking spray and wipe the excess off.

MAKE THE CARAMEL

1. Combine the cream, sugar, butter, and corn syrup in an 8-quart stock pot.
2. Bring the mixture to a boil, stirring constantly. Be careful—it can bubble over very quickly if you aren't paying attention!
3. Cook over medium-high heat, and continue to stir until a candy thermometer reaches 248 degrees. Your caramels will be just beneath the firm ball stage.
4. Remove from the heat and quickly stir in the vanilla and sea salt. Keep in mind that the caramel will continue to cook, even though you have removed it from the heat. The longer you take, the harder your caramel will become.
5. Pour the caramel into the prepared pan and let it cool completely before cutting. This takes about 8 hours.

CARAMEL

4 cups heavy cream

4 cups sugar

¾ cup butter

2 cups light corn syrup

1 Tbsp. vanilla

1 Tbsp. coarse sea salt

CHOCOLATE CARAMELS

RICH AND DECADENT, THESE CARAMELS ARE SURE TO SATISFY EVEN THE MOST DISCERNING CHOCOLATE LOVER.

PREPARE YOUR PAN

1. Spray your jelly roll pan with a thin layer of cooking spray and, using a clean, dry paper towel, wipe the excess off. Make sure you cover the sides and bottom of the pan; this will help prevent the caramels from sticking
2. Trim a piece of parchment paper so it covers the bottom of the pan but has about a 2-inch overhang over the handles.
3. Spray the parchment paper with a light layer of cooking spray and wipe the excess off.

MAKE THE CARAMEL

1. Combine the cream and chocolate chips in an 8-quart stock pot set over medium-low heat. Stir until chocolate is completely melted and smooth.
2. Add in the corn syrup and sugar.
3. Bring the mixture to a boil, stirring constantly. Be careful—it can bubble over very quickly if you aren't paying attention!
4. Cook over medium-high heat and continue to stir until a candy thermometer reaches 248 degrees. This is just beneath the firm ball stage.
5. Remove from heat and quickly stir in the butter. Stir until the butter is completely incorporated.
6. Pour into prepared pan and let cool completely before cutting, about 8 hours.

CARAMEL

4 cups heavy cream

1 lb. good-quality semisweet chocolate chips

2 cups light corn syrup

4 cups sugar

¼ cup butter

BANANA CARAMELS

WE'RE NOT MONKEYING AROUND, THESE BANANA CARAMELS HAVE SWEET A-PEEL!

PREPARE YOUR PAN

1. Spray your jelly roll pan with a thin layer of cooking spray and, using a clean, dry paper towel, wipe the excess off. Make sure you cover the sides and bottom of the pan; this will help prevent the caramels from sticking.
2. Trim a piece of parchment paper so that if just covers the bottom of the pan but has about a 2-inch overhang over the handles.
3. Spray the parchment paper with a light layer of cooking spray and wipe the excess off.

MAKE THE CARAMEL

1. Combine the cream, sugar, butter, and corn syrup in an 8-quart stock pot
2. Bring the mixture to a boil, stirring constantly. Be careful—it can bubble over very quickly if you aren't paying attention!
3. Cook over medium-high heat and continue to stir while boiling until a candy thermometer reaches 248 degrees. This is just beneath the firm ball stage.
4. Remove from heat and quickly stir in your banana flavor. Keep in mind that the caramel will continue to cook even though you have removed it from the heat. The longer you take, the harder your caramel will become.
5. Pour into prepared pan and let cool completely before cutting, about 8 hours.

CARAMEL

4 cups heavy cream

4 cups sugar

¾ cup butter

2 cups light corn syrup

1 Tbsp. banana flavoring

ESPRESSO CARAMELS

RICH ESPRESSO COLLIDES WITH SWEET CARAMEL. I THINK YOU'LL LIKE THEM A LATTE.

PREPARE YOUR PAN

1. Spray your jelly roll pan with a thin layer of cooking spray and, using a clean, dry paper towel, wipe the excess off. Make sure you cover the sides and bottom of the pan; this will help prevent the caramels from sticking.
2. Trim a piece of parchment paper so it covers the bottom of the pan but has about a 2-inch overhang over the handles.
3. Spray the parchment paper with a light layer of cooking spray and wipe the excess off.

MAKE THE CARAMEL

1. Combine the cream, sugar, butter, and corn syrup in an 8-quart stock pot.
2. Bring the mixture to a boil, stirring constantly. Be careful— it can bubble over very quickly if you aren't paying attention!
3. Cook over medium-high heat and continue to stir while boiling until a candy thermometer reaches 248 degrees. This is just beneath the firm ball stage.
4. Remove from heat and quickly stir in your espresso. Keep in mind that the caramel with continue to cook even though you have removed it from the heat. The longer you take, the harder your caramel will become.
5. Pour into prepared pan and either leave them plain or top them off with chocolate-covered espresso beans, crushed biscotti, or crushed spice cookies. Let cool completely before cutting.

CARAMEL

4 cups heavy cream

4 cups sugar

¾ cup butter

2 cups light corn syrup

3 Tbsp. espresso powder dissolved in 2 Tbsp. hot water

THE PIE'S THE LIMIT

INSPIRED BY THE CLASSICS, THESE PIE CARAMELS ARE DELICIOUS ANY WAY YOU SLICE IT.

KEY LIME PIE CARAMELS

THESE ARTISAN CARAMELS START WITH A CRUNCHY GRAHAM CRACKER CRUST, TOPPED WITH A SWEET AND TANGY LIME-FLAVORED CARAMEL. SO AUTHENTIC, YOU MIGHT THINK YOU'RE IN KEY WEST.

PREPARE YOUR OVEN AND YOUR PAN

1. Preheat the oven to 350 degrees.
2. Spray your jelly roll pan with a thin layer of cooking spray and, using a clean, dry paper towel, wipe the excess off. Make sure you cover the sides and bottom of the pan; this will help prevent the caramels from sticking.
3. Trim a piece of parchment paper so it covers the bottom of the pan but has about a 2-inch overhang over the handles.

MAKE THE CRUST

1. Combine all ingredients together and firmly press into prepared pan.
2. Bake at 350 degrees for about 8–10 minutes, or until the edges look golden and the crust becomes fragrant.
3. Remove from the oven and let cool.

MAKE THE CARAMEL

1. Combine the cream, sugar, butter, and corn syrup in an 8-quart stock pot set over medium-high heat.
2. Bring the mixture to a boil, stirring constantly. Be careful—it can bubble over very quickly if you aren't paying attention!
3. Cook over medium-high heat and continue to stir until a candy thermometer reaches 248 degrees. This is just beneath the firm ball stage.
4. Remove from heat and quickly stir in lime extract.
5. Pour over prepared crust and allow to cool completely, for about 8 hours, before cutting.

GRAHAM CRACKER CRUST

2 cups finely crushed graham cracker crumbs

½ cup butter, melted

¼ cup sugar

CARAMEL

4 cups heavy cream

4 cups sugar

¾ cup butter

2 cups light corn syrup

2 Tbsp. lime or Key lime extract

APPLE PIE CARAMELS

HEADY WITH THE FLAVORS OF CRISP APPLES AND WARM SPICES, THESE ARTISAN CARAMELS TASTE LIKE FALL.

PREPARE YOUR OVEN AND YOUR PAN

1. Preheat the oven to 350 degrees.
2. Spray your jelly roll pan with a thin layer of cooking spray and, using a clean, dry paper towel, wipe the excess off. Make sure you cover the sides and bottom of the pan; this will help prevent the caramels from sticking.
3. Trim a piece of parchment paper so it covers the bottom of the pan but has about a 2-inch overhang over the handles.

MAKE THE CRUST

1. Add the sugar and salt to the melted butter and stir. Add in the egg yolks and stir until combined, then add the flour and stir until fully incorporated.
2. Spread your dough into your prepared jelly roll pan. Press down, making sure the layer is even; otherwise the thinner areas will cook faster and have an increased chance of burning.
3. Bake at 350 degrees for about 14 minutes, or until the edges look golden.
4. Remove from the oven and let cool.

MAKE THE CARAMEL

1. Bring the first five ingredients to a boil, stirring constantly until the mixture reaches 248 degrees on a candy thermometer.
2. Remove from heat and stir in the last five ingredients quickly.
3. Pour the caramel over the prepared crust and let cool completely (about 8 hours).

BUTTER COOKIE CRUST

1 cup butter, melted

¾ cup sugar

½ tsp. salt

2 egg yolks, lightly whisked

2 cups flour

CARAMEL

4 cups heavy cream

4 cups sugar

¾ cup butter

2 cups light corn syrup

½ cup boiled apple cider

¾ tsp. salt

1 tsp. vanilla

1 Tbsp. boiled cider

1 tsp. cinnamon

½ tsp. apple pie spice

PUMPKIN PIE CARAMELS

MADE WITH REAL PUMPKIN AND FLAVORED WITH PIE SPICE. THESE ARTISAN CARAMELS TASTE SO MUCH LIKE THE REAL THING YOU'LL BE TEMPTED TO GET A FORK.

PREPARE YOUR OVEN AND YOUR PAN

1. Preheat the oven to 350 degrees.
2. Spray your jelly roll pan with a thin layer of cooking spray and, using a clean, dry paper towel, wipe the excess off. Make sure you cover the sides and bottom of the pan; this will help prevent the caramels from sticking.
3. Trim a piece of parchment paper so it covers the bottom of the pan but has about a 2-inch overhang over the handles.

MAKE THE CRUST

1. Add the sugar and salt to the melted butter and stir. Add in the egg yolks and stir until combined, then add the flour and stir until fully incorporated.
2. Spread your dough into your prepared jelly roll pan. Press down, making sure the layer is even; otherwise the thinner areas will cook faster and have an increased chance of burning.
3. Bake at 350 degrees for about 14 minutes, or until the edges look golden.
4. Remove from the oven and let cool.

MAKE THE CARAMEL

1. Whisk the canned pumpkin into the cream and then pour it into your 8-quart stock pot.
2. Add the butter, corn syrup, and sugar and stir constantly until the mixture reaches 248 degrees on a candy thermometer.
3. Immediately remove from heat and stir in the salt, vanilla, cinnamon, and pumpkin pie spice.
4. Pour the caramel over the prepared crust and let cool completely (about 8 hours).

BUTTER COOKIE CRUST

I cup butter, melted

¾ cup sugar

½ tsp. salt

2 egg yolks, lightly whisked

2 cups flour

CARAMEL

½ cup canned pumpkin

4 cups heavy cream

¾ cup butter

2 cups light corn syrup

4 cups sugar

¾ tsp. salt

I tsp. vanilla

½ tsp. cinnamon

I tsp. pumpkin pie spice

COCONUT CREAM PIE CARAMELS

SWEET TOASTED COCONUT MEETS A COCONUT MILK CARAMEL AND TRANSFORMS THE CLASSIC SOUTHERN DESSERT INTO A MODERN ARTISAN CARAMEL.

PREPARE YOUR OVEN AND YOUR PAN

1. Preheat the oven to 350 degrees.
2. Spray your jelly roll pan with a thin layer of cooking spray and, using a clean, dry paper towel, wipe the excess off. Make sure you cover the sides and bottom of the pan; this will help prevent the caramels from sticking.
3. Trim a piece of parchment paper so it covers the bottom of the pan but has about a 2-inch overhang over the handles.

MAKE THE CRUST

1. Add the sugar and salt to the melted butter and stir. Add in the egg yolks and stir until combined. Then add the flour and stir until fully incorporated.
2. Spread your dough into your prepared jelly roll pan. Press down, making sure the layer is even; otherwise the thinner areas will cook faster and have an increased chance of burning.
3. Bake at 350 degrees for about 14 minutes, or until the edges look golden.
4. Remove from the oven and let cool

PREPARE YOUR TOASTED COCONUT

1. Preheat your oven to 350 degrees
2. Spread enough sweetened coconut to cover the bottom of a jelly roll pan.
3. Bake until golden brown and fragrant, turning/stirring often to prevent burning. Cool and set aside.

BUTTER COOKIE CRUST

1 cup butter, melted

¾ cup sugar

½ tsp. salt

2 egg yolks, lightly whisked

2 cups flour

CARAMEL

4 cups heavy cream

2 cups light corn syrup

4 cups sugar

¾ cup butter

½ cup coconut milk

sweetened shredded coconut

MAKE THE CARAMEL

1. Bring all the ingredients to a boil, stirring constantly until the mixture reaches 248 degrees on a candy thermometer, just under firm ball stage.
2. Remove from heat and pour the caramel over the prepared crust.
3. Top with toasted coconut.
4. Cool completely before cutting.

PECAN PIE CARAMELS

TOASTED PECANS, RICH BOURBON VANILLA CARAMEL, AND A BUTTER COOKIE CRUST. THESE CARAMELS HAVE ALL THE LIKENESS OF YOUR FAVORITE HOLIDAY PIE AND CAN BE ENJOYED ANY TIME OF YEAR.

PREPARE YOUR OVEN AND YOUR PAN

1. Preheat the oven to 350 degrees
2. Spray your jelly roll pan with a thin layer of cooking spray and, using a clean, dry paper towel, wipe the excess off. Make sure you cover the sides and bottom of the pan; this will help prevent the caramels from sticking.
3. Trim a piece of parchment paper so it covers the bottom of the pan but has about a 2-inch overhang over the handles.

MAKE THE CRUST

1. Add the sugar and salt to the melted butter and stir. Add in the egg yolks and stir until combined; then add the flour and stir until fully incorporated.
2. Spread your dough into your prepared jelly roll pan. Press down, making sure the layer is even; otherwise the thinner areas will cook faster and have an increased chance of burning.
3. Bake at 350 degrees for about 14 minutes, or until the edges look golden.
4. Remove from the oven and let cool.

PREPARE THE PECANS

1. Spread about 2 cups of chopped pecan pieces over the base of a jelly roll pan and bake at 350 degrees until fragrant, about 5–7 minutes. Keep a careful eye on them, turning occasionally, because they burn easily.

MAKE THE CARAMEL

1. Bring everything but the salt and vanilla to a boil, stirring constantly until the mixture reaches 248 degrees on a candy thermometer.

BUTTER COOKIE CRUST

1 cup butter, melted

¾ cup sugar

½ tsp. salt

2 egg yolks, lightly whisked

2 cups flour

CARAMEL

4 cups heavy cream

4 cups sugar

¾ cup butter

2 cups light corn syrup

1 Tbsp. sea salt

1 Tbsp. good-quality bourbon vanilla

2. Remove from heat and quickly stir in the sea salt and vanilla.
3. Pour the caramel over the prepared crust and top with toasted pecans. Make sure you press down on them slightly so that they adhere to the caramel.
4. Let cool completely (about 8 hours) before cutting.

BANANA CREAM PIE CARAMELS

CREAMY BANANA CARAMELS GET TOPPED WITH VANILLA WAFER COOKIES AND A WHITE CHOCOLATE DRIZZLE. THE CLASSIC AMERICAN DESSERT IS NOW THE PERFECT ARTISAN CARAMEL.

PREPARE YOUR PAN

1. Spray your jelly roll pan with a thin layer of cooking spray and, using a clean, dry paper towel, wipe the excess off. Make sure you cover the sides and bottom of the pan; this will help prevent the caramels from sticking.
2. Trim a piece of parchment paper so it covers the bottom of the pan but has about a 2-inch overhang over the handles.
3. Spray the parchment paper with a light layer of cooking spray and wipe the excess off.

MAKE THE CARAMEL

1. Combine the cream, sugar, butter, and corn syrup in an 8-quart stock pot.
2. Bring the mixture to a boil, stirring constantly. Be careful—it can bubble over very quickly if you aren't paying attention!
3. Cook over medium-high heat and continue to stir until a candy thermometer reaches 248 degrees. This is just beneath the firm ball stage.
4. Remove from heat and quickly stir in the banana flavoring.
5. Pour into prepared pan and top with vanilla wafer cookies. Let cool completely.
6. Melt chocolate candy according to directions on package. Drizzle over caramel and let cool until hard.

CARAMEL

4 cups heavy cream

4 cups sugar

¾ cup butter

2 cups light corn syrup

1 Tbsp. banana flavoring

1 (11-oz.) pkg. vanilla wafer cookies

white chocolate melting wafers

CHOCOLATE LOVERS

MILK CHOCOLATE, DARK CHOCOLATE, WHITE CHOCOLATE, MELTED CHOCOLATE, CHOCOLATE CHUNKS, CHOCOLATE DRIZZLE.

DID I MENTION THAT THIS SECTION IS DEDICATED TO CHOCOLATE?

S'MORES CARAMELS

CRUNCHY GRAHAM CRACKERS, CHOCOLATE CARAMEL, AND MARSHMALLOWS. A NEW TWIST ON A CLASSIC CAMPFIRE TREAT.

PREPARE YOUR PAN

1. Spray your jelly roll pan with a thin layer of cooking spray and, using a clean, dry paper towel, wipe the excess off. Make sure you cover the sides and bottom of the pan; this will help prevent the caramels from sticking.
2. Trim a piece of parchment paper so it covers the bottom of the pan but has about a 2-inch overhang over the handles.
3. Spray the parchment paper with a light layer of cooking spray and wipe the excess off.
4. Place a layer of graham crackers along the bottom of the pan, trying to cover as much as possible.

MAKE THE CARAMEL

1. Combine the cream and chocolate chips in an 8-quart stock pot set over medium-low heat. Stir until chocolate is completely melted and smooth.
2. Add in the corn syrup and sugar.
3. Bring the mixture to a boil, stirring constantly. Be careful— it can bubble over very quickly if you aren't paying attention!
4. Cook over medium-high heat and continue to stir until a candy thermometer reaches 248 degrees. This is just beneath the firm ball stage.
5. Remove from heat and quickly stir in the butter. Stir until the butter is completely incorporated.
6. Pour into prepared pan and top with mini marshmallows, slightly pressing down to make sure they adhere to the caramel.
7. Let cool completely before cutting, about 8 hours.

CARAMEL

4 cups heavy cream

1 lb. good-quality semisweet chocolate chips

2 cups light corn syrup

4 cups sugar

¼ cup butter

1 (10-oz.) bag mini marshmallows

CHOCOLATE ORANGE CARAMELS

THESE CARAMELS ARE THE PERFECT MARRIAGE OF RICH, CREAMY CHOCOLATE AND LUSCIOUS ORANGE.

PREPARE YOUR PAN

1. Spray your jelly roll pan with a thin layer of cooking spray and, using a clean, dry paper towel, wipe the excess off. Make sure you cover the sides and bottom of the pan; this will help prevent the caramels from sticking.
2. Trim a piece of parchment paper so it covers the bottom of the pan but has about a 2-inch overhang over the handles.
3. Spray the parchment paper with a light layer of cooking spray and wipe the excess off.

MAKE THE CARAMEL

1. Combine the cream and chocolate chips in an 8-quart stock pot set over medium-low heat. Stir until chocolate is completely melted and smooth.
2. Add in the corn syrup and sugar.
3. Bring the mixture to a boil, stirring constantly. Be careful—it can bubble over very quickly if you aren't paying attention!
4. Cook over medium-high heat and continue to stir until a candy thermometer reaches 248 degrees. This is just beneath the firm ball stage.
5. Remove from heat and quickly stir in the butter and the orange extract. Stir until the butter is completely incorporated.
6. Pour into prepared pan and let cool completely before cutting, about 8 hours.
7. Top each piece with candied orange peel before wrapping.

CARAMEL

4 cups heavy cream

1 lb. good-quality milk chocolate chips

2 cups light corn syrup

4 cups sugar

¼ cup butter

2 Tbsp. orange extract

candied orange peel for topping

MOCHA COOKIE CARAMELS

THE ESPRESSO ENHANCES THE RICHNESS OF THE CHOCOLATE. WHEN TOPPED WITH CRUSHED CHOCOLATE SANDWICH COOKIES, THESE CARAMELS GO FROM ARTISAN TO DOWNRIGHT DECADENT.

PREPARE YOUR PAN

1. Spray your jelly roll pan with a thin layer of cooking spray and, using a clean, dry paper towel, wipe the excess off. Make sure you cover the sides and bottom of the pan; this will help prevent the caramels from sticking.
2. Trim a piece of parchment paper so it covers the bottom of the pan but has about a 2-inch overhang over the handles.
3. Spray the parchment paper with a light layer of cooking spray and wipe the excess off.

MAKE THE CARAMEL

1. Combine the cream and chocolate chips in an 8-quart stock pot set over medium-low heat. Stir until chocolate is completely melted and smooth.
2. Add in the corn syrup, sugar, and espresso.
3. Bring the mixture to a boil, stirring constantly. Be careful—it can bubble over very quickly if you aren't paying attention!
4. Cook over medium-high heat and continue to stir until a candy thermometer reaches 248 degrees. This is just beneath the firm ball stage.
5. Remove from heat and quickly stir in the butter until it is completely incorporated.
6. Pour into prepared pan and top with chopped cookies. Let cool completely, for about 8 hours.
7. Melt candy according to package and drizzle over caramel. Let cool to harden.

CARAMEL

4 cups heavy cream

1 lb. good-quality semisweet chocolate chips

2 cups light corn syrup

4 cups sugar

3 Tbsp. espresso powder dissolved in 2 Tbsp. hot water

¼ cup butter

2 cups chopped chocolate sandwich cookies

good-quality chocolate candy melting wafers

HOT, HOT CHOCOLATE CARAMELS

DON'T LET THE SWEET LITTLE MARSHMALLOWS FOOL YOU: THIS HOT CHOCOLATE CARAMEL HAS A SPICY SIDE.

PREPARE YOUR PAN

1. Spray your jelly roll pan with a thin layer of cooking spray and, using a clean, dry paper towel, wipe the excess off. Make sure you cover the sides and bottom of the pan; this will help prevent the caramels from sticking.
2. Trim a piece of parchment paper so it covers the bottom of the pan but has about a 2-inch overhang over the handles.
3. Spray the parchment paper with a light layer of cooking spray and wipe the excess off.

MAKE THE CARAMEL

1. Combine the cream and hot cocoa in an 8-quart stock pot set over medium-high heat.
2. When the chocolate is fully incorporated, add the butter, sugar, and corn syrup.
3. Bring the mixture to a boil, stirring constantly. Be careful—it can bubble over very quickly if you aren't paying attention!
4. Cook over medium-high heat and continue to stir until a candy thermometer reaches 248 degrees. This is just beneath the firm ball stage.
5. Remove from heat and quickly stir in cayenne pepper.
6. Pour into prepared pan and top with marshmallows. Cool completely before cutting, about 8 hours.

CARAMEL

4 cups heavy cream

⅔ cup good-quality hot cocoa

¾ cup butter

4 cups sugar

2 cups light corn syrup

1 tsp. cayenne pepper

mini marshmallows or "Mallow Bits"

RASPBERRY AND WHITE CHOCOLATE CARAMELS

TART RASPBERRY CARAMEL GETS DRIZZLED IN CREAMY WHITE CHOCOLATE, MAKING THEM AS PRETTY TO LOOK AT AS THEY ARE DELICIOUS TO EAT.

PREPARE YOUR PAN

1. Spray your jelly roll pan with a thin layer of cooking spray and, using a clean, dry paper towel, wipe the excess off. Make sure you cover the sides and bottom of the pan; this will help prevent the caramels from sticking.
2. Trim a piece of parchment paper so it covers the bottom of the pan but has about a 2-inch overhang over the handles.
3. Spray the parchment paper with a light layer of cooking spray and wipe the excess off.

MAKE THE CARAMEL

1. Combine the cream, sugar, butter, and corn syrup in an 8-quart stock pot.
2. Bring the mixture to a boil, stirring constantly. Be careful— it can bubble over very quickly if you aren't paying attention!
3. Cook over medium-high heat and continue to stir until a candy thermometer reaches 248 degrees. This is just beneath the firm ball stage.
4. Remove from heat and quickly stir in raspberry flavor.
5. Pour into prepared pan and let cool completely.
6. Melt chocolate candy according to package and drizzle or spread over caramel. Allow to harden before cutting.

CARAMEL

4 cups heavy cream

4 cups sugar

¾ cup butter

2 cups light corn syrup

2 Tbsp. natural raspberry flavor

white chocolate candy
melting wafers

BANANA CHOCOLATE WALNUT CARAMELS

BANANA CARAMELS TOPPED WITH CHOCOLATE CHUNKS AND WALNUTS. IN ONE WORD: CHUNKALICIOUS!

PREPARE YOUR PAN

1. Spray your jelly roll pan with a thin layer of cooking spray and, using a clean, dry paper towel, wipe the excess off. Make sure you cover the sides and bottom of the pan; this will help prevent the caramels from sticking.
2. Trim a piece of parchment paper so it covers the bottom of the pan but has about a 2-inch overhang over the handles.
3. Spray the parchment paper with a light layer of cooking spray and wipe the excess off.

MAKE THE CARAMEL

1. Combine the cream, sugar, butter, and corn syrup in an 8-quart stock pot.
2. Bring the mixture to a boil, stirring constantly. Be careful—it can bubble over very quickly if you aren't paying attention!
3. Cook over medium-high heat and continue to stir until a candy thermometer reaches 248 degrees. This is just beneath the firm ball stage.
4. Remove from heat and quickly stir in the banana flavoring.
5. Pour into prepared pan and top with walnuts and chocolate chunks. Let cool completely before cutting, about 8 hours.

CARAMEL

4 cups heavy cream

4 cups sugar

¾ cup butter

2 cups light corn syrup

1 Tbsp. banana flavoring

1 cup chopped walnuts

1 cup chocolate chunks

SPECIALTY DESSERTS

FROM TIRAMISU TO ROOT BEER FLOATS, SOME OF YOUR FAVORITE DESSERTS GET A CARAMEL MAKEOVER, AND THE RESULTS ARE DELICIOUS!

RED VELVET CARAMELS

RED VELVET COOKIE CRUST AND CREAM CHEESE FLAVORED CARAMEL, MAKE THESE ARTISAN CARAMELS AS DELECTABLE AS THE CAKES THEY'RE NAMED AFTER.

PREPARE YOUR OVEN AND YOUR PAN

1. Preheat the oven to 350 degrees.
2. Spray your jelly roll pan with a thin layer of cooking spray and, using a clean, dry paper towel, wipe the excess off. Make sure you cover the sides and bottom of the pan; this will help prevent the caramels from sticking.
3. Trim a piece of parchment paper so it covers the bottom of the pan but has about a 2-inch overhang over the handles.

MAKE THE CRUST

1. Add the sugar and salt to the melted butter and stir. Add in the eggs and stir until combined.
2. Add the flour, cocoa powder, and red velvet bakery emulsion and stir until fully incorporated.
3. Spread your dough into your prepared jelly roll pan. Press down, making sure the layer is even; otherwise the thinner areas will cook faster and have an increased chance of burning.
4. Bake at 350 degrees for about 14 minutes, or until the edges look golden.
5. Remove from the oven and let cool.

MAKE THE CARAMEL

1. Combine the sugar, cream, butter, and corn syrup in an 8-quart stock pot set over medium-high heat.
2. Bring the mixture to a boil, stirring constantly. Be careful—it can bubble over very quickly if you aren't paying attention!
3. Cook over medium-high heat and continue to stir until a candy thermometer reaches 248 degrees. This is just beneath the firm ball stage.
4. Remove from heat and quickly stir in cream cheese emulsion.
5. Pour over prepared crust and allow to cool completely before cutting.

RED VELVET COOKIE CRUST

1 cup butter, melted
¾ cup sugar
½ tsp. salt
2 eggs, lightly whisked
1½ cups flour
¼ cup good-quality cocoa powder
1 Tbsp. red velvet bakery emulsion

CARAMEL

4 cups sugar
4 cups heavy cream
¾ cup butter
2 cups light corn syrup
2 Tbsp. cream cheese bakery emulsion

CHOCOLATE CHIP CHEESECAKE CARAMELS

INSPIRED BY THE POPULAR DESSERT, THESE CARAMELS CALL FOR CHEESECAKE EMULSION, WHICH GIVES THE CARAMEL A TRULY AUTHENTIC CHEESECAKE FLAVOR.

PREPARE YOUR OVEN AND YOUR PAN

1. Preheat the oven to 350 degrees.
2. Spray your jelly roll pan with a thin layer of cooking spray and, using a clean, dry paper towel, wipe the excess off. Make sure you cover the sides and bottom of the pan; this will help prevent the caramels from sticking.
3. Trim a piece of parchment paper so it covers the bottom of the pan but has about a 2-inch overhang over the handles.

MAKE THE CRUST

1. Add the sugars and salt to the melted butter and stir. Add in the egg yolks and stir until combined; then add the flour and cinnamon and stir until fully incorporated. Finally, gently stir in the mini chocolate chips.
2. Spread your dough into your prepared jelly roll pan. Press down, making sure the layer is even; otherwise the thinner areas will cook faster and have an increased chance of burning.
3. Bake at 350 degrees for about 14 minutes, or until the edges look golden.
4. Remove from the oven and let cool.

MAKE THE CARAMEL

1. Combine the sugar, cream, butter, and corn syrup in an 8-quart stock pot set over medium-high heat.
2. Bring the mixture to a boil, stirring constantly. Be careful— it can bubble over very quickly if you aren't paying attention!
3. Cook over medium-high heat and continue to stir until a

CHOCOLATE CHIP COOKIE CRUST

½ cup brown sugar

¼ cup sugar

½ tsp. salt

1 cup butter, melted

2 egg yolks, lightly whisked

2 cups flour

¼ tsp. cinnamon

½ cup mini chocolate chips

CARAMEL

4 cups sugar

4 cups heavy cream

¾ cup butter

2 cups light corn syrup

2 Tbsp. cheesecake emulsion

candy thermometer reaches 248 degrees. This is just beneath the firm ball stage.
4. Remove from heat and quickly stir in cheesecake emulsion.
5. Pour over prepared crust and let cool 8 hours before cutting.

STRAWBERRY CHEESECAKE CARAMELS

GRAHAM CRACKER CRUST AND STRAWBERRY CHEESECAKE CARAMEL. YOU'LL BE TEMPTED TO SAVE THESE FOR SPECIAL OCCASIONS (LIKE DAYS ENDING IN 'Y').

PREPARE YOUR OVEN AND YOUR PAN

1. Preheat the oven to 350 degrees.
2. Spray your jelly roll pan with a thin layer of cooking spray and, using a clean, dry paper towel, wipe the excess off. Make sure you cover the sides and bottom of the pan; this will help prevent the caramels from sticking.
3. Trim a piece of parchment paper so it covers the bottom of the pan but has about a 2-inch overhang over the handles.

MAKE THE CRUST

1. Combine all ingredients together and firmly press into prepared pan.
2. Bake at 350 degrees for about 8–10 minutes, or until the edges look golden and the crust becomes fragrant.
3. Remove from the oven and let cool.

MAKE THE CARAMEL

1. Combine the sugar, cream, butter, preserves, and corn syrup in an 8-quart stock pot set over medium-high heat.
2. Bring the mixture to a boil, stirring constantly. Be careful— it can bubble over very quickly if you aren't paying attention!
3. Cook over medium-high heat and continue to stir until a candy thermometer reaches 248 degrees. This is just beneath the firm ball stage.
4. Remove from heat and quickly stir in cheesecake emulsion. Pour over prepared crust and top with diced dried strawberries. Allow to cool completely for 8 hours before cutting.

GRAHAM CRACKER CRUST

2 cups finely crushed graham cracker crumbs

½ cup butter, melted

¼ cup sugar

CARAMEL

4 cups sugar

4 cups heavy cream

¾ cup butter

½ cup all-natural strawberry preserves

2 cups light corn syrup

2 Tbsp. cheesecake emulsion

TIRAMISU CARAMELS

SWEET CREAM CARAMEL FLAVORED WITH ESPRESSO AND TOPPED WITH LADYFINGERS AND A DUSTING OF COCOA. THESE CARAMELS WILL MAKE YOU SAY "TI AMO!"

PREPARE YOUR PAN

1. Spray your jelly roll pan with a thin layer of cooking spray and, using a clean, dry paper towel, wipe the excess off. Make sure you cover the sides and bottom of the pan; this will help prevent the caramels from sticking.
2. Trim a piece of parchment paper so it covers the bottom of the pan but has about a 2-inch overhang over the handles.
3. Spray the parchment paper with a light layer of cooking spray and wipe the excess off.

MAKE THE CARAMEL

1. Combine the cream, creamer, sugar, butter, and corn syrup in an 8-quart stock pot.
2. Bring the mixture to a boil, stirring constantly. Be careful—it can bubble over very quickly if you aren't paying attention!
3. Cook over medium-high heat and continue to stir until a candy thermometer reaches 248 degrees. This is just beneath the firm ball stage.
4. Remove from heat and quickly stir in the espresso.
5. Pour into prepared pan and top them with ladyfingers. Let cool completely before cutting. Dust with cocoa powder.

CARAMEL

2 cups heavy cream

2 cups sweet cream-flavored liquid coffee creamer

4 cups sugar

¾ cup butter

2 cups light corn syrup

3 Tbsp. espresso powder dissolved in 2 Tbsp. hot water

1 (7-oz.) pkg. ladyfingers

BAKEWELL TART CARAMELS

A MODERN TWIST TO A TRADI-
TIONAL ENGLISH DESSERT. THIS
ARTISAN CARAMEL COMBINES A
DELICIOUS BUTTER COOKIE CRUST
WITH SWEET ALMOND AND TART
RASPBERRY.

PREPARE YOUR OVEN AND YOUR PAN

1. Preheat the oven to 350 degrees.
2. Spray your jelly roll pan with a thin layer of cooking spray and, using a clean, dry paper towel, wipe the excess off. Make sure you cover the sides and bottom of the pan; this will help prevent the caramels from sticking.
3. Trim a piece of parchment paper so it covers the bottom of the pan but has about a 2-inch overhang over the handles.

MAKE THE CRUST

1. Add the sugar and salt to the melted butter and stir. Add in the egg yolks and stir until combined, then add the flours and stir until fully incorporated.
2. Spread your dough into your prepared jelly roll pan. Press down, making sure the layer is even; otherwise the thinner areas will cook faster and have an increased chance of burning.
3. Bake at 350 degrees for about 14 minutes, or until the edges look golden.
4. Remove from the oven and let cool.

MAKE THE CARAMEL

1. Combine cream, sugar, butter, and corn syrup in an 8-quart stock pot. Set over medium heat, stirring constantly, until the mixture reaches 248 degrees on a candy thermometer. This is just beneath the firm ball stage.
2. Remove from heat and stir in almond extract.

BUTTER COOKIE CRUST

I cup butter, melted

¾ cup sugar

½ tsp. salt

2 egg yolks, lightly whisked

I½ cups flour

½ cup almond flour

CARAMEL

4 cups heavy cream

4 cups sugar

¾ cup butter

2 cups light corn syrup

2 Tbsp. pure almond extract

I cup raspberry jammy bits

I cup sliced almonds

3. Pour the caramel over the prepared crust and evenly sprinkle jammy bits over the top.
4. Cool completely for 8 hours before cutting, and then top each cut piece with sliced almonds.

SAMOA CARAMELS

CRUNCHY COOKIE, GOLDEN CARAMEL, TOASTED COCONUT, AND CHOCOLATE DRIZZLE: YOUR FAVORITE COOKIE COMBINATION IS ABOUT TO BECOME YOUR FAVORITE CARAMEL!

PREPARE YOUR OVEN AND YOUR PAN

1. Preheat the oven to 350 degrees.
2. Spray your jelly roll pan with a thin layer of cooking spray and, using a clean, dry paper towel, wipe the excess off. Make sure you cover the sides and bottom of the pan; this will help prevent the caramels from sticking.
3. Trim a piece of parchment paper so it covers the bottom of the pan but has about a 2-inch overhang over the handles.

MAKE THE CRUST

1. Add the sugar and salt to the melted butter and stir. Add in the egg yolks and stir until combined; then add the flour and stir until fully incorporated.
2. Spread your dough into your prepared jelly roll pan. Press down, making sure the layer is even; otherwise the thinner areas will cook faster and have an increased chance of burning.
3. Bake at 350 degrees for about 14 minutes, or until the edges look golden.
4. Remove from the oven and let cool.

MAKE THE CARAMEL

1. Bring all the ingredients to a boil, stirring constantly until the mixture reaches 248 degrees on a candy thermometer. Just under the firm ball stage.
2. Pour the caramel over the prepared crust and immediately top with toasted coconut (see opposite page).

BUTTER COOKIE CRUST

1 cup butter, melted

¾ cup sugar

½ tsp. salt

2 egg yolks, lightly whisked

2 cups flour

CARAMEL

4 cups heavy cream

2 cups light corn syrup

4 cups sugar

¾ cup butter

3. Let cool completely (about 8 hours). Drizzle with chocolate if desired (see opposite page).

TO TOAST COCONUT

1. Spread an even layer of sweetened shredded coconut over the bottom of a jelly roll pan. Bake at 350 degrees until golden brown and fragrant. Stir often, because coconut will burn easily.

TO MAKE THE CHOCOLATE DRIZZLE

1. In a saucepan set over medium-low heat, melt 8 ounces of semisweet chocolate chips together with 1 teaspoon corn syrup and ½ cup butter, and stir until smooth. Let cool slightly and place in a decorating bag or parchment triangle. Cut off a small triangle from the bottom tip of your decorator bag. Let melted chocolate drip onto the caramel and move in a sweeping motion as it does so. Cool completely before cutting and wrapping the caramels.

ROOT BEER CARAMELS

MADE WITH ROOT BEER SYRUP AND SWEET CREAM, THESE ARTISAN CARAMELS ARE FULL OF THE CLASSIC SODA SHOP FLAVOR.

PREPARE YOUR PAN

1. Spray your jelly roll pan with a thin layer of cooking spray and, using a clean, dry paper towel, wipe the excess off. Make sure you cover the sides and bottom of the pan; this will help prevent the caramels from sticking.
2. Trim a piece of parchment paper so it covers the bottom of the pan but has about a 2-inch overhang over the handles.
3. Spray the parchment paper with a light layer of cooking spray and wipe the excess off.

MAKE THE CARAMEL

1. Combine the cream, creamer, sugar, butter, corn syrup, and root beer syrup in an 8-quart stock pot.
2. Bring the mixture to a boil, stirring constantly. Be careful—it can bubble over very quickly if you aren't paying attention!
3. Cook over medium-high heat and continue to stir until a candy thermometer reaches 248 degrees. This is just beneath the firm ball stage.
4. Remove from heat and quickly pour into prepared pan.
5. Let cool completely before cutting, about 8 hours.

CARAMEL

2 cups heavy cream

2 cups sweet cream coffee creamer

4 cups sugar

¾ cup butter

2 cups light corn syrup

½ cup root beer syrup

AROUND THE WORLD

TAKE A JOURNEY WITH YOUR TASTE BUDS!
INSPIRATION AND INGREDIENTS FOR THESE
CARAMELS CAME FROM ALL OVER THE WORLD.

MATCHA GREEN TEA CARAMELS

KEEPING WITH THE TRADITION OF BALANCING BITTER AND SWEET, THESE MATCHA GREEN TEA CARAMELS WITH WHITE CHOCOLATE GIVE YOU THE FEELING OF BEING AT A JAPANESE TEA CEREMONY RIGHT IN YOUR OWN HOME.

PREPARE YOUR PAN

1. Spray your jelly roll pan with a thin layer of cooking spray and, using a clean, dry paper towel, wipe the excess off. Make sure you cover the sides and bottom of the pan; this will help prevent the caramels from sticking.
2. Trim a piece of parchment paper so it covers the bottom of the pan but has about a 2-inch overhang over the handles.
3. Spray the parchment paper with a light layer of cooking spray and wipe the excess off.

MAKE THE CARAMEL

1. In an 8-quart stock pot set over medium heat whisk the green tea powder and the cream until fully incorporated.
2. Next, add sugar, butter, and corn syrup.
3. Bring the mixture to a boil, stirring constantly. Be careful—it can bubble over very quickly if you aren't paying attention!
4. Cook over medium-high heat and continue to stir until a candy thermometer reaches 248 degrees. This is just beneath the firm ball stage.
5. Remove from heat and pour into prepared pan.
6. Let cool completely before cutting.
7. Melt white chocolate wafers according to package.
8. Once caramels are cut, spread a small amount of white chocolate on top of each piece and allow to cool to harden.

CARAMEL

½ cup matcha green tea powder

4 cups heavy cream

4 cups sugar

¾ cup butter

2 cups light corn syrup

white chocolate melting wafers

PISTACHIO AND CARDAMOM CARAMELS

REMINISCENT OF TRADITIONAL INDIAN AND SOUTH ASIAN DESSERTS, WE'VE PAIRED PISTACHIOS WITH CARDAMOM FOR A TRULY EXOTIC ARTISAN CARAMEL.

PREPARE YOUR PAN

1. Spray your jelly roll pan with a thin layer of cooking spray and, using a clean, dry paper towel, wipe the excess off. Make sure you cover the sides and bottom of the pan; this will help prevent the caramels from sticking.
2. Trim a piece of parchment paper so it covers the bottom of the pan but has about a 2-inch overhang over the handles.
3. Spray the parchment paper with a light layer of cooking spray and wipe the excess off.

MAKE THE CARAMEL

1. Combine the cream, sugar, butter, and corn syrup in an 8-quart stock pot.
2. Bring the mixture to a boil, stirring constantly. Be careful— it can bubble over very quickly if you aren't paying attention!
3. Cook over medium-high heat and continue to stir until a candy thermometer reaches 248 degrees. This is just beneath the firm ball stage.
4. Remove from heat and quickly stir in cardamom.
5. Pour into prepared pan and top with pistachios.
6. Let cool completely before cutting, about 8 hours.

CARAMEL

4 cups heavy cream

4 cups sugar

¾ cup butter

2 cups light corn syrup

1 Tbsp. freshly ground cardamom seeds

1 cup shelled raw pistachios, whole or chopped

FIORI DI SICILIA CARAMELS

TRANSLATED IT MEANS "FLOWERS OF SICILY" AND IT IS A LUSCIOUS COMBINATION OF CITRUS, VANILLA, AND FLORAL AROMA. TOP OFF THESE CARAMELS WITH CRUSHED ALMOND BISCOTTI FOR A NUTTY CRUNCH THAT'S "MOLTO BENE!"

PREPARE YOUR PAN

1. Spray your jelly roll pan with a thin layer of cooking spray and, using a clean, dry paper towel, wipe the excess off. Make sure you cover the sides and bottom of the pan; this will help prevent the caramels from sticking.
2. Trim a piece of parchment paper so it covers the bottom of the pan but has about a 2-inch overhang over the handles.
3. Spray the parchment paper with a light layer of cooking spray and wipe the excess off.

MAKE THE CARAMEL

1. Combine the cream, sugar, butter, and corn syrup in an 8-quart stock pot.
2. Bring the mixture to a boil, stirring constantly. Be careful—it can bubble over very quickly if you aren't paying attention!
3. Cook over medium-high heat and continue to stir until a candy thermometer reaches 248 degrees. This is just beneath the firm ball stage.
4. Remove from heat and quickly stir in Fiori di Sicilia.
5. Pour into prepared pan and top with crushed biscotti. Let cool completely before cutting, about 8 hours.

CARAMEL

4 cups heavy cream

4 cups sugar

¾ cup butter

2 cups light corn syrup

1 Tbsp. pure Fiori di Sicilia

2 cups crushed almond biscotti

STOUT AND PRETZEL CARAMELS

FULL OF RICH STOUT FLAVOR AND TOPPED WITH CRUNCHY, SALTY PRETZELS, IT'S LIKE BEING AT YOUR FAVORITE PUB WITHOUT HAVING TO WAIT FOR A TABLE.

PREPARE YOUR PAN

1. Spray your jelly roll pan with a thin layer of cooking spray and, using a clean, dry paper towel, wipe the excess off. Make sure you cover the sides and bottom of the pan; this will help prevent the caramels from sticking.
2. Trim a piece of parchment paper so it covers the bottom of the pan but has about a 2-inch overhang over the handles.
3. Spray the parchment paper again with a light layer of cooking spray and wipe the excess off.

PREPARE YOUR STOUT

1. Pour an entire can of stout into a small saucepan, set over medium heat, and bring to a boil. Cook until reduced to ½ cup.

MAKE THE CARAMEL

1. Combine the cream, sugar, butter, corn syrup, and stout in an 8-quart stock pot.
2. Bring the mixture to a boil, stirring constantly. Be careful—it can bubble over very quickly if you aren't paying attention!
3. Cook over medium-high heat and continue to stir until a candy thermometer reaches 248 degrees. This is just beneath the firm ball stage.
4. Remove from heat and quickly stir in your sea salt.
5. Pour into prepared pan and top with pretzels. Let cool completely before cutting, about 8 hours.

CARAMEL

4 cups heavy cream

4 cups brown sugar

¾ cup butter

2 cups light corn syrup

I (14.9-oz.) can stout

I tsp. sea salt

EARL GREY AND LEMON CARAMELS

THE PERFECT COMBINATION OF AUTHENTIC EARL GREY TEA, CARAMEL, AND A LEMON SUGAR COOKIE CRUST. OFFICIALLY MAKING ANYTIME TEA TIME!

PREPARE YOUR OVEN AND YOUR PAN

1. Preheat the oven to 350 degrees.
2. Spray your jelly roll pan with a thin layer of cooking spray and, using a clean, dry paper towel, wipe the excess off. Make sure you cover the sides and bottom of the pan; this will help prevent the caramels from sticking.
3. Trim a piece of parchment paper so it covers the bottom of the pan but has about a 2-inch overhang over the handles.

MAKE THE CRUST

1. Using clean hands, rub the lemon zest into the sugar—this will release the oil in the peel, making a more fragrant sugar. It should resemble wet sand.
2. Add the sugar and salt to the melted butter and stir. Add in the egg yolks and stir until combined. Add the flour and stir until fully incorporated.
3. Spread your dough into your prepared jelly roll pan. Press down, making sure the layer is even; otherwise the thinner areas will cook faster and have an increased chance of burning.
4. Bake at 350 degrees for about 14 minutes, or until the edges look golden.
5. Remove from the oven and let cool.

STEEPING THE TEA

1. Place just over 4 cups of cream in a sauce pan with 6–8 good-quality, loose leaf tea bags and bring to a boil.
2. Once it reaches boiling, turn it off and let it steep for about 30 minutes.

LEMON COOKIE CRUST

zest from I lemon

¾ cup sugar

½ tsp. salt

I cup butter, melted

2 egg yolks, lightly whisked

2 cups flour

CARAMEL

4 cups tea infused heavy cream

2 cups light corn syrup

4 cups sugar

¾ cup butter

3. Strain the cream to remove the "skin" that forms, as well as the tea bags.

MAKE THE CARAMEL

1. Bring all the ingredients to a boil stirring constantly until the mixture reaches 248 degrees on a candy thermometer, until just under the firm ball stage.
2. Pour the caramel over the prepared crust and cool completely before cutting.

SAFFRON AND BLOOD ORANGE OLIVE OIL CARAMELS

SAFFRON AND BLOOD ORANGE ARE THE PERFECT COMBINATION, AND WHILE THEY ARE TYPICALLY USED FOR SAVORY DISHES, IN CARAMEL FORM THEY ARE TRULY SUPERB.

PREPARE YOUR OVEN AND YOUR PAN

1. Preheat the oven to 350 degrees.
2. Spray your jelly roll pan with a thin layer of cooking spray and, using a clean, dry paper towel, wipe the excess off. Make sure you cover the sides and bottom of the pan; this will help prevent the caramels from sticking.
3. Trim a piece of parchment paper so it covers the bottom of the pan but has about a 2-inch overhang over the handles.

MAKE THE CRUST

1. Using clean hands, rub the orange zest into the sugar—this will release the oil in the peel making a more fragrant sugar.
2. Add the sugar and salt to the olive oil and stir. Add the eggs and stir until combined.
3. Add the flour and stir until fully incorporated.
4. Spread your dough into your prepared jelly roll pan. Press down, making sure the layer is even; otherwise the thinner areas will cook faster and have an increased chance of burning.
5. Bake at 350 degrees for about 14 minutes, or until the edges look golden.
6. Remove from the oven and let cool.

STEEPING THE SAFFRON

1. Place just over 4 cups of cream in a sauce pan with 1 table-spoon of saffron strands and bring to a boil.
2. Once it reaches boiling, turn it off and let it steep for about 30 minutes. Your cream will turn a gorgeous golden color.
3. Strain the cream to remove the saffron and the "skin" that forms.

BLOOD ORANGE OLIVE OIL COOKIE CRUST

1 cup sugar

¼ tsp. salt

½ cup blood orange-infused olive oil or extra virgin olive oil

2 eggs, lightly whisked

2 cups flour

zest from 1 blood orange

CARAMEL

4 cups saffron-infused heavy cream

2 cups light corn syrup

4 cups sugar

¾ cup butter

MAKE THE CARAMEL

1. Bring all the ingredients to a boil, stirring constantly until the mixture reaches 248 degrees on a candy thermometer. Just under firm ball stage.
2. Pour the caramel over the prepared crust and cool completely.

BLACKBERRY AND GINGER CARAMELS

BLACKBERRY GETS PAIRED WITH CANDIED GINGER, MAKING THESE ARTISAN CARAMELS THE PERFECT COMBINATION OF SWEET AND SPICY.

PREPARE YOUR PAN

1. Spray your jelly roll pan with a thin layer of cooking spray and, using a clean, dry paper towel, wipe the excess off. Make sure you cover the sides and bottom of the pan; this will help prevent the caramels from sticking.
2. Trim a piece of parchment paper so it covers the bottom of the pan but has about a 2-inch overhang over the handles.
3. Spray the parchment paper with a light layer of cooking spray and wipe the excess off.

MAKE THE CARAMEL

1. Combine the cream, sugar, butter, and corn syrup in an 8-quart stock pot.
2. Whisk in blackberry preserves.
3. Bring the mixture to a boil, stirring constantly. Be careful—it can bubble over very quickly if you aren't paying attention!
4. Cook over medium-high heat and continue to stir until a candy thermometer reaches 248 degrees. This is just beneath the firm ball stage.
5. Remove from heat and pour into prepared pan.
6. Cool completely.
7. Cut caramel into squares and top with candied ginger.

CARAMEL

4 cups heavy cream

4 cups sugar

¾ cup butter

2 cups light corn syrup

½ cup blackberry preserves

diced candied ginger

HOLIDAYS AND MORE

THINK OUTSIDE THE (GIFT) BOX.

IN ADDITION TO THE CLASSICS, HERE ARE A
FEW EXTRA FLAVORS TO INSPIRE SOME NEW
HOLIDAY TRADITIONS.

HONEY WALNUT CARAMELS

INSPIRED BY THE TRADITIONAL CAKES MADE DURING PASSOVER, WE'VE TAKEN CRUNCHY WALNUTS AND SWEET HONEY AND COMBINED THEM FOR AMAZING ARTISAN CARAMEL.

PREPARE YOUR PAN

1. Spray your jelly roll pan with a thin layer of cooking spray and, using a clean, dry paper towel, wipe the excess off. Make sure you cover the sides and bottom of the pan; this will help prevent the caramels from sticking.
2. Trim a piece of parchment paper so it covers the bottom of the pan but has about a 2-inch overhang over the handles.
3. Spray the parchment paper with a light layer of cooking spray and wipe the excess off.

MAKE THE CARAMEL

1. Combine the cream, sugar, butter, corn syrup, and honey in an 8-quart stock pot.
2. Bring the mixture to a boil, stirring constantly. Be careful—it can bubble over very quickly if you aren't paying attention!
3. Cook over medium-high heat and continue to stir until a candy thermometer reaches 248 degrees. This is just beneath the firm ball stage.
4. Remove from heat and quickly stir in orange extract and cinnamon.
5. Pour into prepared pan, top with walnuts, and let cool completely before cutting, about 8 hours.

CARAMEL

4 cups heavy cream

4 cups sugar

¾ cup butter

2 cups light corn syrup

½ cup real honey

1 tsp. orange extract

½ tsp. cinnamon

1¾ cups chopped walnuts

PFEFFERNÜSSE CARAMELS

INSPIRED BY THE GERMAN HOLIDAY COOKIES, THESE ARTISAN CARAMELS ARE MADE WITH RICH MOLASSES AND FLAVORED WITH SPICES LIKE FRESHLY CRACKED PEPPERCORN, CINNAMON, AND CLOVES.

PREPARE YOUR PAN

1. Spray your jelly roll pan with a thin layer of cooking spray and, using a clean, dry paper towel, wipe the excess off. Make sure you cover the sides and bottom of the pan; this will help prevent the caramels from sticking.
2. Trim a piece of parchment paper so it covers the bottom of the pan but has about a 2-inch overhang over the handles.
3. Spray the parchment paper with a light layer of cooking spray and wipe the excess off.

MAKE THE CARAMEL

1. Combine the cream, sugar, butter, molasses, and corn syrup in an 8-quart stock pot.
2. Bring the mixture to a boil, stirring constantly. Be careful—it can bubble over very quickly if you aren't paying attention!
3. Cook over medium-high heat and continue to stir until a candy thermometer reaches 248 degrees. This is just beneath the firm ball stage.
4. Remove from heat and quickly stir in vanilla, salt, and spices.
5. Pour into prepared pan and let cool completely before cutting, about 8 hours.
6. For an authentic pfeffernüsse look, dust with powdered sugar.

CARAMEL

4 cups heavy cream

4 cups sugar

¾ cup butter

½ cup molasses

2 cups light corn syrup

1 tsp. vanilla

¾ tsp. each: salt, ginger, cardamom, and nutmeg

1½–2 tsp. freshly cracked peppercorn

1 tsp. cinnamon

½ tsp. ground cloves

EGGNOG CARAMELS

WITH ITS RICH FLAVOR AND HINT OF NUTMEG, THESE ARTISAN CARAMELS ARE SURE TO BECOME A DELICIOUS HOLIDAY TRADITION.

PREPARE YOUR PAN

1. Spray your jelly roll pan with a thin layer of cooking spray and, using a clean, dry paper towel, wipe the excess off. Make sure you cover the sides and bottom of the pan; this will help prevent the caramels from sticking.
2. Trim a piece of parchment paper so it covers the bottom of the pan but has about a 2-inch overhang over the handles.
3. Spray the parchment paper with a light layer of cooking spray and wipe the excess off.

MAKE THE CARAMEL

1. Combine the cream, eggnog, sugar, butter, and corn syrup in an 8-quart stock pot.
2. Bring the mixture to a boil, stirring constantly. Be careful—it can bubble over very quickly if you aren't paying attention!
3. Cook over medium-high heat and continue to stir until a candy thermometer reaches 248 degrees. This is just beneath the firm ball stage.
4. Remove from heat and quickly stir in eggnog flavor and nutmeg.
5. Pour into prepared pan and let cool completely before cutting, about 8 hours.

CARAMEL

2 cups heavy cream

2 cups good-quality eggnog

4 cups sugar

¾ cup butter

2 cups light corn syrup

1 Tbsp. eggnog flavor

½ tsp. nutmeg

PEPPERMINT MOCHA CARAMELS

SWEET PEPPERMINT GETS PAIRED WITH RICH CHOCOLATY MOCHA. YOUR FAVORITE COFFEE HOUSE BEVERAGE IS NOW AN ARTISAN CARAMEL.

PREPARE YOUR PAN

1. Spray your jelly roll pan with a thin layer of cooking spray and, using a clean, dry paper towel, wipe the excess off. Make sure you cover the sides and bottom of the pan; this will help prevent the caramels from sticking.
2. Trim a piece of parchment paper so it covers the bottom of the pan but has about a 2-inch overhang over the handles.
3. Spray the parchment paper with a light layer of cooking spray and wipe the excess off.

MAKE THE CARAMEL

1. Combine the cream and chocolate chips in an 8-quart stock pot set over medium-low heat. Stir until chocolate is completely melted and smooth.
2. Add in the corn syrup, sugar, and espresso.
3. Bring the mixture to a boil, stirring constantly. Be careful—it can bubble over very quickly if you aren't paying attention!
4. Cook over medium-high heat and continue to stir until a candy thermometer reaches 248 degrees. This is just beneath the firm ball stage.
5. Remove from heat and quickly stir in the butter. Stir until the butter is completely incorporated.
6. Pour into prepared pan and top with crushed candy canes. Let cool completely.

CARAMEL

4 cups heavy cream

1 lb. good-quality semisweet chocolate chips

2 cups light corn syrup

4 cups sugar

3 Tbsp. espresso powder dissolved in 2 Tbsp. hot water

¼ cup butter

2 cups crushed candy canes

LEMON LAVENDER CARAMELS

THE CREAM IS INFUSED WITH LAVENDER, AND THE SHORTBREAD CRUST HAS A HINT OF LEMON. TOP THEM OFF WITH TINY LAVENDER BUDS AND YOU HAVE A CARAMEL THAT IS SURE TO DELIGHT ALL YOUR SENSES.

PREPARE YOUR OVEN AND YOUR PAN

1. Preheat the oven to 350 degrees
2. Spray your jelly roll pan with a thin layer of cooking spray and, using a clean, dry paper towel, wipe the excess off. Make sure you cover the sides and bottom of the pan; this will help prevent the caramels from sticking.
3. Trim a piece of parchment paper so it covers the bottom of the pan but has about a 2-inch overhang over the handles.

MAKE THE CRUST

1. Using clean hands, rub the lemon zest into the sugar—this will release the oil in the peel making a more fragrant sugar.
2. Add the sugar and salt to the melted butter and stir. Add in the egg yolks and stir until combined, then add the flour and stir until fully incorporated.
3. Spread your dough into your prepared jelly roll pan. Press down, making sure the layer is even; otherwise the thinner areas will cook faster and have an increased chance of burning.
4. Bake at 350 degrees for about 14 minutes, or until the edges look golden.
5. Remove from the oven and let cool.

STEEPING THE LAVENDER

1. Place just over 4 cups (you will lose some after straining) of cream in a sauce pan with 2 tablespoons lavender buds and bring to a boil.
2. Once it begins to boil, turn the heat off and let steep for about 30 minutes.
3. Strain the cream to remove the "skin" that forms and all the buds.

BUTTER COOKIE CRUST

zest from 1 lemon

¾ cup sugar

½ tsp. salt

1 cup butter, melted

2 egg yolks, lightly whisked

2 cups flour

CARAMEL

4 cups lavender-infused heavy cream

2 cups light corn syrup

4 cups sugar

¾ cup butter

MAKE THE CARAMEL

1. Bring all the ingredients to a boil, stirring constantly until the mixture reaches 248 degrees on a candy thermometer, until just under the firm ball stage.
2. Pour the caramel over the prepared crust and cool completely.
3. After cutting the caramels, top with dried lavender buds.

FRENCH TOAST CARAMELS WITH BACON

THESE ARTISAN CARAMELS ARE FLAVORED WITH CINNAMON AND PURE MAPLE SYRUP, AND ARE TOPPED WITH REAL CRUMBLED BACON. YES, BACON. THEY'RE LIKE BREAKFAST, ONLY BETTER.

PREPARE YOUR PAN

1. Spray your jelly roll pan with a thin layer of cooking spray and, using a clean, dry paper towel, wipe the excess off. Make sure you cover the sides and bottom of the pan; this will help prevent the caramels from sticking.
2. Trim a piece of parchment paper so it covers the bottom of the pan but has about a 2-inch overhang over the handles.
3. Spray the parchment paper with a light layer of cooking spray and wipe the excess off.

PREPARE THE BACON

1. Measure out enough real bacon crumbles to cover the bottom of a jelly roll pan (about 10 oz.).
2. Place the bacon in a frying pan set over medium-high heat.
3. Fry until bacon is crispy and transfer to a plate lined with a paper towel.

MAKE THE CARAMEL

1. Combine the cream, sugar, butter, corn syrup, and maple syrup in an 8-quart stock pot.
2. Bring the mixture to a boil, stirring constantly. Be careful—it can bubble over very quickly if you aren't paying attention!
3. Cook over medium-high heat, continue to stir, until a candy thermometer reaches 248 degrees.
4. Remove from heat and quickly stir in your vanilla, syrup, salt, and cinnamon. Keep in mind that the caramel will continue to cook even though you have removed it from the heat. The longer you take the harder your caramel will become.

CARAMEL

4 cups heavy cream

4 cups sugar

¾ cup butter

2 cups light corn syrup

½ cup pure maple syrup

1 tsp. vanilla

1 Tbsp. pure maple syrup

¾ tsp. salt

1 tsp. cinnamon

about 12 oz. real bacon crumbles

5. Pour into prepared pan and immediately top with cooked, crumbled bacon.
6. Let cool completely before cutting.

CINNAMON ROLL CARAMELS

BUTTERY SWEET DOUGH FLAVOR AND CINNAMON COMBINE TO GIVE YOU AN AUTHENTIC CINNAMON ROLL FLAVOR. THEY'RE SO GOOD, YOU'LL BE TEMPTED TO HAVE THEM FOR BREAKFAST.

PREPARE YOUR PAN

1. Spray your jelly roll pan with a thin layer of cooking spray and, using a clean, dry paper towel, wipe the excess off. Make sure you cover the sides and bottom of the pan; this will help prevent the caramels from sticking.
2. Trim a piece of parchment paper so it covers the bottom of the pan but has about a 2-inch overhang over the handles.
3. Spray the parchment paper with a light layer of cooking spray and wipe the excess off.

MAKE THE CARAMEL

1. Combine the sugar, cream, butter, and corn syrup in an 8-quart stock pot set over medium-high heat.
2. Bring the mixture to a boil, stirring constantly. Be careful— it can bubble over very quickly if you aren't paying attention!
3. Cook over medium-high heat and continue to stir until a candy thermometer reaches 248 degrees. This is just beneath the firm ball stage.
4. Remove from heat and quickly stir in buttery sweet dough bakery emulsion and cinnamon.
5. Pour into prepared pan. Cool completely.
6. Melt chocolate candy wafers according to directions on package. Drizzle over caramel and let cool until hard.

CARAMEL

4 cups sugar

4 cups heavy cream

¾ cup butter

2 cups light corn syrup

2 Tbsp. buttery sweet dough bakery emulsion

1 Tbsp. cinnamon

white chocolate melting wafers

INDEX

ACKNOWLEDGMENTS

I have been making caramel for several years now—experimenting with flavors, creating new recipes, failing and succeeding in ways I had never dreamed possible. It is a huge honor for me to share these recipes with all of you. To guide you through the process and help you experience caramel is a truly unique and artisan capacity.

I am so grateful for my family. There are no words to express the amount of love I have for you. Miguel, you have tried hundreds of caramels and helped me wash hundreds of dishes. You have been my sanity, my strength, and my support. Every dream I have is bigger and brighter with you in it. Connor and Addison, you love me unconditionally and there is no greater gift. Even with stressed out, kitchen disaster, caramel madness, you have shown me patience and given me hugs when I needed them most. If nothing else, I hope I have shown you that any dream is possible.

For my parents, who have been almost as excited as I am for this book to get finished, your love and support means more than I ever tell you. And my brother Jeff, who has almost as many crazy ideas as I do, I promise I will someday create a chicken and waffle caramel for you!

Danica—thank you for making my stuff look so good.

Maria, Melissa, Carrie—your late-night, joke telling, selfie-sharing, un-official editing has saved me throughout this entire process. I am lucky to have you in my little gang. xoxox

So many of my friends, near and far, have been with me on this sweet journey. You have listened and sampled and I am eternally grateful for all of your support.

For all of my Firefly Confections fans, friends, and patrons—THANK YOU. You have been there since the beginning. You have suggested flavor combinations, offered to be guinea pigs, and asked me on a regular basis to make a cook book. Here you go. I would not have done this if it weren't for all of you.

And last, but not least—thank you to Joanna Barker, Hannah Ballard, and Cedar Fort, Inc. You guided me along the way and helped me turn a crazy idea into a gorgeous reality.

ABOUT THE AUTHOR

Baking has always been a large part of Sandy's life, with sweet memories of time spent in the kitchen alongside her great-grandmother. So it's no surprise that baking for her family and friends, which started as a hobby after her son was born, eventually turned into a thriving business.

In addition to her growing list of celebrity clients, Sandy has also donated countless sweets for Operation Shower, a non-profit organization that provides baby showers to military wives whose husbands are deployed.

Sandy currently resides in Crystal Lake, Illinois, with her husband and two kids.

You can order from her at www.FireflyConfections.com

And follow her on social media:

Facebook: Firefly Confections

Twitter: @sandysbaking

Instagram: @sandysbaking

Pinterest: Sandy Fregin-Arevalo

COOKING MEASUREMENT EQUIVALENTS

Cups	Tablespoons	Fluid Ounces
⅛ cup	2 Tbsp.	1 fl. oz.
¼ cup	4 Tbsp.	2 fl. oz.
⅓ cup	5 Tbsp. + 1 tsp.	
½ cup	8 Tbsp.	4 fl. oz.
⅔ cup	10 Tbsp. + 2 tsp.	
¾ cup	12 Tbsp.	6 fl. oz.
1 cup	16 Tbsp.	8 fl. oz.

Cups	Fluid Ounces	Pints/Quarts/Gallons
1 cup	8 fl. oz.	½ pint
2 cups	16 fl. oz.	1 pint = ½ quart
3 cups	24 fl. oz.	1½ pints
4 cups	32 fl. oz.	2 pints = 1 quart
8 cups	64 fl. oz.	2 quarts = ½ gallon
16 cups	128 fl. oz.	4 quarts = 1 gallon

Other Helpful Equivalents

1 Tbsp.	3 tsp.
8 oz.	½ lb.
16 oz.	1 lb.

METRIC MEASUREMENT EQUIVALENTS

Approximate Weight Equivalents

Ounces	Pounds	Grams
4 oz.	¼ lb.	113 g
5 oz.		142 g
6 oz.		170 g
8 oz.	½ lb.	227 g
9 oz.		255 g
12 oz.	¾ lb.	340 g
16 oz.	1 lb.	454 g

Approximate Volume Equivalents

Cups	US Fluid Ounces	Milliliters
⅛ cup	1 fl. oz.	30 ml
¼ cup	2 fl. oz.	59 ml
½ cup	4 fl. oz.	118 ml
¾ cup	6 fl. oz.	177 ml
1 cup	8 fl. oz.	237 ml

Other Helpful Equivalents

½ tsp.	2½ ml	
1 tsp.	5 ml	
1 Tbsp.	15 ml	

PRAISE FOR *ARTISAN CARAMELS*

"Sandy's book is a must-have for all caramel lovers. You will fall in love with the innovative and delicious caramel flavors like strawberry cheesecake and pistachio-cardamom! Learn the art of creating artisan caramels for your family and friends!"

COURTNEY WHITMORE
Author of *Push-Up Pops,*
Candy Making For Kids, & *Frostings*

"Sandy's Salted Vanilla Bean caramels are melt-in-your-mouth creamy and can be summed up in one word: addicting. I'm in love with her new cookbook and am excited about being able to recreate one of my favorite indulgent treats! You seriously have to try them… but don't say I didn't warn you."

MARIAH LEESON
Giggles Galore

"Filled with tons of creative recipes, *Artisan Caramels* is a MUST-HAVE for those who love sweets! You'll quickly learn that Sandy's caramels are addictive and make the perfect gift!

MELISSA CHAMBERS
Melissa Creates

RESOURCES

KING ARTHUR FLOUR

King Arthur Flour is a great resource for many of the flavorings, chocolate, and toppings used in this book (such as dried fruit and "art bits").

They also offer a variety of tools and bakeware.
www.KingArthurFlour.com

NUTS.COM

In addition to their wide variety of nuts and dried fruits, Nuts.com also has a large selections of quality teas, including Earl Grey and Matcha, as used in this book.
www.nuts.com

SUR LA TABLE

Sur la Table offers a wide variety of kitchen equipment and bakeware, such large stock pots and candy thermometers.
www.surlatable.com

COSTCO

Costco is a member's only wholesale warehouse. I have earned my membership in the sugar, butter, and heavy cream I have purchased over the years!
www.costco.com

AMAZON

Amazon is your one-stop shop for hard-to-find items such as toppings, flavors, and specialty items. If you can't find it anywhere else, you are sure to find it on Amazon.
www.amazon.com

0 26575 14429 1